Tip It In

Daisy Hawkins

hed in 2026 by
ood House Press
Clinton Street
, NY 14224

d in the United States of America

Library of Congress Cataloging-in-Publication Data:
Names: Hawkins, Daisy, author. | Teng, Lee, illustrator.
Title: Tip it in / written by Daisy Hawkins. Top pit / written by Daisy Hawkins, illustrated by Lee Teng.
Description: Buffalo, NY : Norwood House Press, 2026. | Series: Phonics all-stars: phase 2 |
Identifiers: ISBN 9781978577879 (pbk.) | ISBN 9781978577886 (library bound) | ISBN 9781978577893 (ebook)
Subjects: LCSH: Reading–Phonetic method–Juvenile literature. | English language–Phonetics–Juvenile literature. | Cooking–Juvenile literature. | Excavation–Juvenile literature.
Classification: LCC LB1573.3 H395 2026 | DDC 372.465–dc23

CPSIA compliance information: Batch #CW26NHP: For further information contact Norwood House Press at 1-800-237-9932.

Tap it.

Pat it.

Tip it, Mag.
Tip it in a pan.

Tip, tip.

Dip it, Dan.
Dip it in a pan.

Dip, dip.

Sip it, Sam.

Top Pit

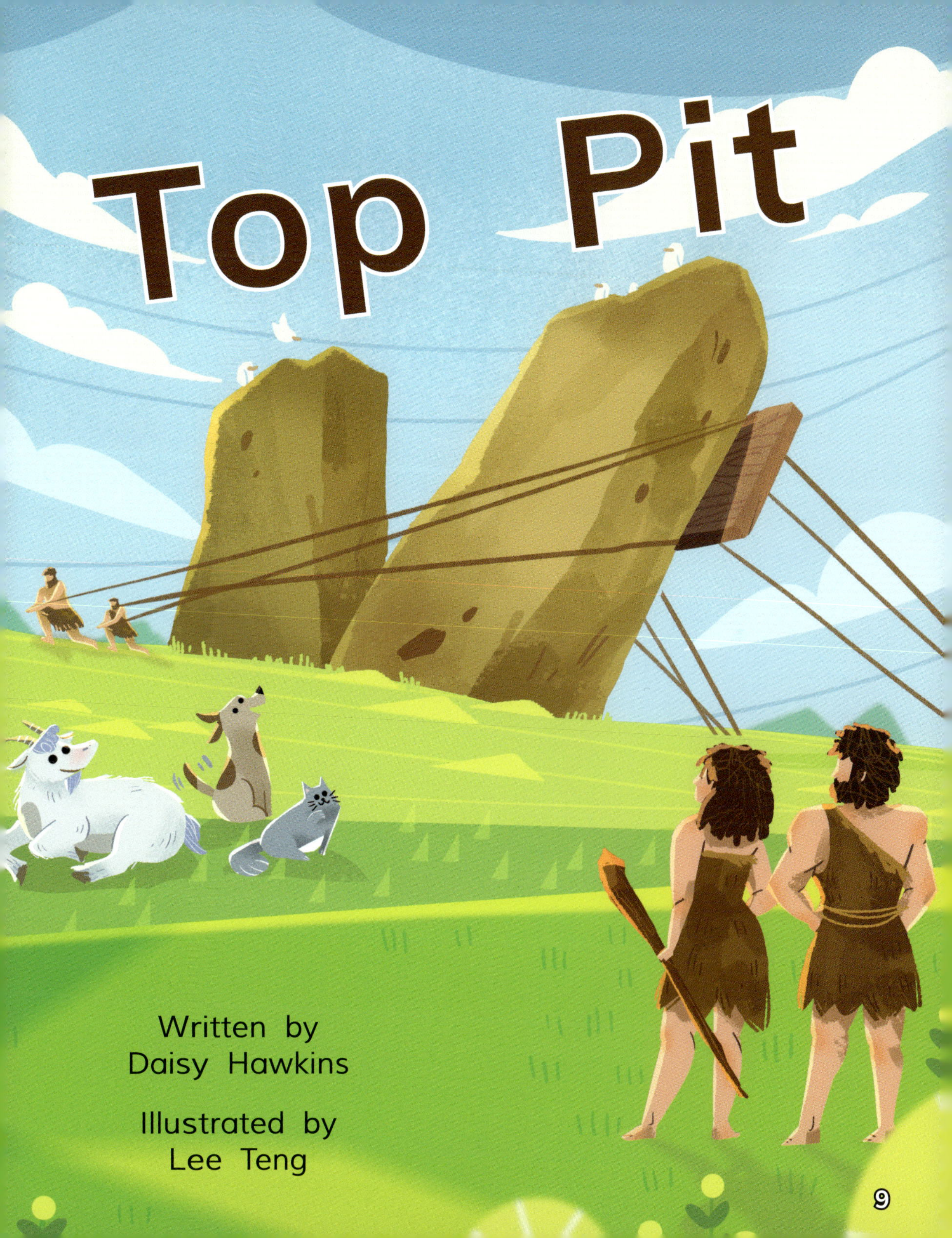

Written by
Daisy Hawkins

Illustrated by
Lee Teng

Kim can dig the pit.

Cam can not
dig the pit.

Cam is sad.

Can Cam top Kim?
Can Cam dig
a top pit?

Cam got a dog,
a cat, a kid ...

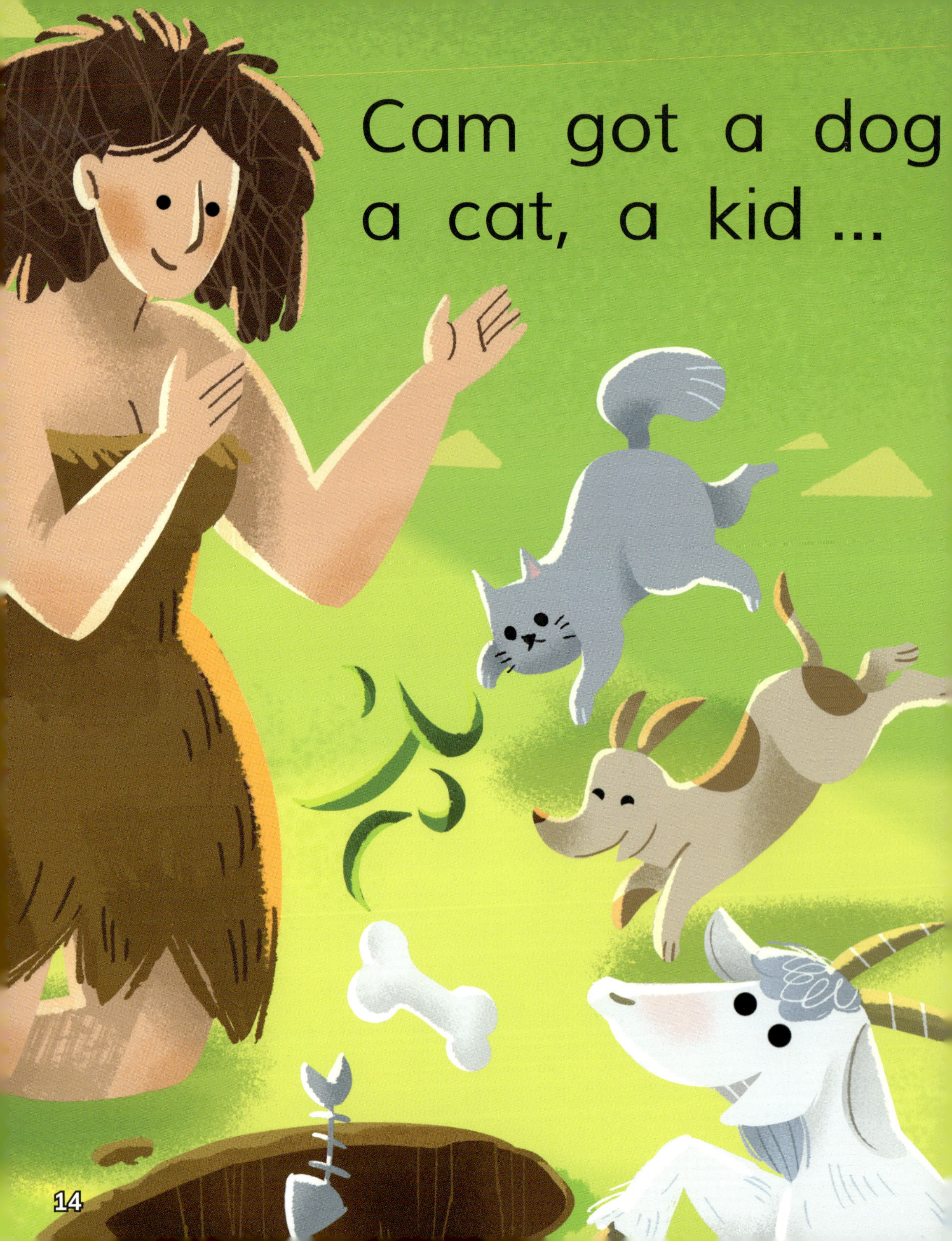

Dig, Cam! Dig!

Cam did it!
Top pit, Cam.